little Pearls

By Lisa Guy

Illustrated by Cameron Shields

This book is not intended as a substitute for advice from a trained professional.

Library of Congress Control Number: 2023919968
ISBN # 979-8-9887106-4-6
Illustrations by Cameron Shields
Graphic Art and Design by Cameron Shields and Kate Summers

This book is available at a special discount when purchased in bulk for educational purposes. For details, contact the author through the website Pearls4Parents.com
Printed in the United States of America
First printing February 2024

To my mother, who has always made me feel respected and loved.

~Lisa Guy

To my father and mother, who taught me the value of perspective in both drawing and life.

~Cameron Shields

Our home makes me feel
loved and snug ~

Like the warmth and
comfort of a tender hug.

The soothing rhythm of
our nights and days ~

calms me down
in many ways.

Music makes
my heart sing ~

with the playful lullabies
your voice will bring.

Eating good food
makes me healthy
and strong ~

and we both know
I'll be grown before long.

My habits are
what I do each day ~

They shape my life
in many ways.

When you smile at me,
I smile back ~

It makes me feel happy,
and that's a fact!

Sometimes
I am happy,
and other times
I'm not ~

Emotions
can change quickly,
they make me feel a lot.

My friends are
fun to be with,
and we treat
each other well ~

with visits to the
park and beach,
spending time
collecting shells.

I can practice sharing
while playing
with my friends ~

When we explore
our toys together,
the fun times never end.

Let's go outside
and enjoy the day ~

We can run and hop
and skip and play!

I learn best when
you talk to me ~

and put away the
technology.

Our family sticks together ~

We are a team, forever.

If you show me respect,
I'll respect you as well ~

We'll form a strong bond,
as time will soon tell.

Trying new things
can be fulfilling ~

Help me
spark my curiosity
and explore,
if I am willing!

I can do many things
to help myself
and others too ~

Give me opportunities
and you will see it's true.

Questions for Discussion

Children benefit when we get to know them

1. What makes you feel safe and loved?

2. I wonder, what can you do to help your body feel calm?

3. I love it when I hear you sing! Can we sing a song together? Can we sing fast? Slow? With a silly voice?

4. What are some foods you like to eat that keep your body healthy and strong?

5. Did you know that a habit is something we do every day without thinking – like saying "thank you" when someone does something nice? Can you think of any habits you have?

6. What makes you smile? Can I see a beautiful smile light up your face? What happens if you smile when you don't feel happy? Do you think it might change how you feel?

7. Do you remember a time when you felt mad? Sad? Angry? Happy? Excited? Surprised? Did you know we can have lots of feelings that can change quickly or stay with us for a while?

8. How can friends treat each other well? Can they work together to collect shells at the beach? Take turns on the playground? Be kind to each other?

9. Is it hard for you to share your things with others? Do you remember feeling good when someone shared with you?

10. I wonder what we can do together when we go outside to play?

11. Did you know it is good to take time off from electronics so we can enjoy our family and friends? Taking breaks lets our brain think about new things and explore the real world. It also gives us time to spend with the people we love.

12. What are some things that our family does to help each other?

13. How can we show our respect and love to our family and friends?

14. What are some things you are curious about, or would like to explore?

15. Helping is kind. Tell me about the things you do at home to help your family.

www.ingramcontent.com/pod-product-compliance
Lightning Source LLC
Chambersburg PA
CBHW040521120726
48010CB00005B/202
9798988710646